BOONVILLE and BEYOND:
An Upstate Sampler

by

William L. Crosten

A North Country Books Monograph

Published by
North Country Books, Inc.
Utica, New York

North Country Books, Publisher
18 Irving Place, Utica, New York 13501-5618

ISBN 0-932052-82-7

Library of Congress

To the Memory of

Clark and Hildegarde Layng and Jessie Layng Howland
who introduced the Crosten family to the North Country in 1938

FOREWORD

The photographs in this book are centered on a bit of country that I have known and enjoyed for over fifty years. North of Utica and west of the Adirondacks it typifies in many respects that part of rural New York known as Upstate. Earlier times in this area were liberally pictured in Ronald Ryder's evocative books entitled *Black Cotton Stockings* and *The Way It Was*. With a bow to those classics, the present collection is offered as one man's look at the way it is there today.

In the making of these photographs a few were planned in advance; the majority were shot on the wing as I came upon scenes that struck my eye and looked as if they would play well on film. In either case I was at pains to let the subject matter speak for itself without intrusion of any stage management or without trying, as the current saying goes, to "make a statement." Observers, of course, may take the pictures as they will. For my part, I had two aims in mind: to compose and expose the scenes in such a way as to bring out whatever of atmosphere or emotional tone they happened to have, and to produce a variety of images which, taken together, might give the viewer a certain sense of the region with some inkling of its style of everyday life.

—W.L.C.

1 Sign formerly on Route 46 north of Rome

1

2

3

4

6

7

8

9

10

12

13

14

15

16

17

19

21

22

23

25

26

27

28

29

30

31

32

33

34

35

36

37

38

39

40

41

42

43

44

45

46

47

48

49

50

51

52

54

ABOUT THE PHOTOGRAPHER

William Crosten is an Iowan by birth, a musician and college teacher by profession, a photographer by avocation and a resident of upstate New York by preference.

As a teacher he held appointments at the University of Iowa, Columbia University, and finally at Stanford University where he served as chairman of its music department for twenty-seven years.

Along the way, while still at Columbia, he and his wife were introduced to the North Country and liked what they saw. In fact, they liked it so well that, upon retiring from Stanford, they moved back to New York to a home in the country outside of Boonville. There they became active in environmental work for the Town and County, and he, for his own pleasure, began a photographic exploration of Upstate which has continued to the present and of which this volume is a sample.